The *NEW* Soap Makers Cookbook
Making Cold Process Soap from Scratch

By: Zakia Ringgold

The New Soap Makers Cookbook – Making Cold Process Soap from Scratch
By Zakia Ringgold

All rights reserved. No part of this book may be reproduced in whole or in part in any form by any means without the express written consent of the author. Requests for permission to reproduce portions of this book should be addressed to **zakia@livesoapschool.com**.

Limits of Liability and Disclaimer of Warranty: This book is strictly for informational and educational purposes. The author and/or publisher shall have neither liability nor responsibility for errors, omissions or for any loss or damage claimed to be related to the information contained in this book.
Copyright © 2018 Zakia Ringgold
All rights reserved.

ISBN: 1983654663
ISBN-13: 978-1983654664

DEDICATION

This book is dedicated to my daughters Nyla and Paige. You continue to inspire and challenge me to be better on a daily basis. It is through your eyes that I see possibility and creativity. Thank You!

To my mom, who brought my initial soaping supplies in an effort to get me out of my funk by any means necessary. You continue to give my soap as gifts to anyone who will take them, you are my true investor and real life hero. Thank You!

To my family and friends who have stuck with me when the only thing I wanted to discuss was the latest and greatest creation, thank you for the listening ear and encouraging words. There are far too many to list and at a risk of leaving someone out I simply say, Thank You!

To my live streaming, digital, social media, Soap Nation I consider you my front row. I thank each of you for tuning in, tapping the screen, sharing the broadcast and even trolling me (in a good way).

Finally for anyone who dared to dream out loud, keep doing it! You motivate the rest of us to just give it a shot and keep going, Thank You!

WHY I WROTE THIS BOOK

This book is a follow-up to my first book "The New Soap Makers Cookbook – Ingredients for Success". As readers got their hands on that book they began asking for more resources on the process to make soap from scratch...at home. My goal with this book is to provide you easy to follow instructions so that you don't have to spend months wading through books, videos and blogs filled with industry terminology and clever marketing that gets you further away from actually getting started.

In "The New Soap Makers Cookbook – Making Cold Process Soap from Scratch", you will get exactly what you need to get started making your own soap at home. You will know what to buy, what to avoid, how to create and customize your own recipes and a step by step blueprint of the cold process soap making process.

I want you to be confident, not overwhelmed.

I want you to be educated, not marketed.

If you want to learn how to make soap, read on. I want you to make your own soap at home so you know every ingredient in your family's skincare and possibly start your own handcrafted soap making business.

This cookbook is a "no-fluff" Zone. If you want to learn the history of soap, Google it. If you want to learn specific SAP values, search on YouTube. If you want elaborate pictures, search for "Soap" on Instagram.

Table of Contents

Cold Process Soap Basics	2
Supplies You Need	5
Ingredients Make the Maker	7
Lye aka Sodium Hydroxide	9
Scenting Your Soap	11
Additives	16
Recipes Create Balance	19
Color Creates Character	22
Terms & Acronyms You Should Know	25
Time, Temperature and Trace	27
Preparing to Make Soap	30
The Steps To Make Soap	32
Get Yourself a Soap Notebook	35
Troubleshooting Problems	36
Part II Cold Process Soap Recipes	39
Basic Soapers Recipe 3 for 3	40
Simple Soap	41
Lots O' Lather	42
Essential Bar	43
White Soap	45
Charcoal Soap	46
Poppy Exfoliation	48

Clay Soap	50
Cup O' Joe	52
Sea Salt Spa Escape	53
Final Thoughts for New Soap Makers	55
Stay Connected	58
About the Author	59
Additional Reading	60

How To Use This Book

This book is written to introduce you to soap making using the cold process method.

Beginner and Never Made Soap
If you have never made soap before, I recommend reading from beginning to end and dog earing pages to review later. Reading it in this manner will give you a solid foundation of important concepts to be successful.

I've Got Everything and I Know the Process
You may have watched a ton a videos or read several blogs and you are just ready to get started. You have all of your supplies and you are looking for some good recipes. If you understand the process, you can go right to Part II for some tried and true recipes.

Curious
If you are just curious, go through the table of contents, find something that interests you and get right to it.

There is no right or wrong way to use this book. I take that back, the absolute wrong way to use this book is to read it and never apply any of it. You must commit to actually doing something in your own soap pot with the information you have learned. Otherwise, it's just another book. We don't want that, I want you to make soap from scratch!

CHAPTER 1
Cold Process Soap Basics

Whatever your reason is for getting started, I'd like to be one of the first people to welcome you to the world of handcrafted natural soap. While it is easy to quickly get overwhelmed, it's even easier to get started with cold process soap making. Hopefully this book will reduce your overwhelm and increase your confidence. Many people take up soap making to start a new hobby, express their creativity, treat skin conditions or to start their own business. The key is to constantly work on it and understand how everything works together.

This process is often referred to as cold pressed or the traditional method. When you hear the term cold process, what comes to mind? If you are like others you may assume it has something to do with a cold temperature. The name is very misleading because the temperatures are extremely hot and there is nothing cold about it.

The name cold process actually stems from the fact that there is no external heat used to force the soap making process. In cold process you are relying on the heat and constant contact of your ingredients to force the soaping process. This is the opposite of hot process soap making which uses the heat from a crock pot or stovetop to force the soap making process.

People often shy away from cold process soap due to the use of sodium hydroxide. However once you are comfortable working with it, you will see there was nothing to fear. We will cover this more in chapter 4.

Simplicity

Cold process soap is a very straight forward method. You complete 6 phases: prepare, measure, mix, mold, cut and cure. I am understating a bit here but it can be as simple or complex as you make it. This complexity will become even more apparent as you delve deeper into the craft. Remember curiosity fuels creativity so if you find yourself doing 20 steps to achieve what can be done in 2, you have definitely crossed over into the complex.

Fluidity & Creativity

Due to the fluid consistency of the soap batter it is easy to work with and create any design you desire. You can work at thin consistencies all the way up to super thick pudding textures. This fluidity makes cold process soap a great method when starting out. No other soap making method offers the ability to express your creativity like the cold process method. Embeds, swirls, layers and more are all possible with cold process soap.

Cure Time

Cold process soap has the longest curing period of all of the soap making options. After you make your soap, you have to wait up to eight weeks before you can actually use it. During this time the bar becomes harder and milder. Just like wine, cold process soap only gets better with time.

You didn't buy this book for all the extra, so let's get right to it with the supplies you will need to get started making soap.

CHAPTER 2
Supplies You Need

What you need in order to make soap can be broken into two distinct categories: Supplies and Ingredients. You can go cheap/used on most supplies but you must look for quality in the tools you will use repeatedly. Get a quality stick blender. The stick blender is the magic wand in the soap making process and you will be happy you invested here.

Many of the supplies that you will need to get started making soap can be found right in your kitchen or garage. There is one rule that you must adhere to here: ***if you use it for soap, it can only be used for soap going forward***. I wouldn't want you to have the taste of soap in your family's favorite casserole. So please adhere to this rule. If you need to procure these supplies, start at local garage sales, second hand stores, consignment shops, thrift shops or discount stores. If all else fails there is an abundance of online sites where you can find what you need.

You do not need the most expensive gadgets and gizmos to get started. Save your money for ingredients. If you absolutely must go online to shop I have created a shopping list as a starting point but you can do your own research to find bargains.

You can access the shopping list with links at: ***https://livesoapschool.com/suppliestomakesoap***

Supplies Needed
- ☐ Reliable kitchen scale that measures in grams and ounces
- ☐ Heat resistant mixing bowls to measure and melt your oils
- ☐ Measuring cup to weigh your lye
- ☐ Thermometer to check temperatures
- ☐ Heat resistant pitcher to create your lye solution
- ☐ 3 to 4 Silicone Spatulas for stirring and scraping the bowls
- ☐ Mixing Bowls
- ☐ Mold to set your cold process soap, these can be plastic or silicone
- ☐ Stick blender to mix lye solution and oils

Let's quickly discuss your choice of molds. Virtually anything can be used as a soap mold. You can use old drawers, yogurt containers, plastic storage boxes and even old milk cartons. If you don't have a lot of money to get started consider up-cycling things around the house. You will need to line them with freezer paper or plastic bags to assist with releasing the hardened soap but you can get really creative with your choice of molds.

Many online suppliers offer a wealth of wooden, plastic and silicone molds. I have not had much success with plastic molds and typically work with silicone and wooden molds. These are specially crafted for making soap and you can find them priced from all ends of the spectrum from basic and inexpensive to custom crafted and very expensive. If you are prepared to buy a professional mold do some research, read the reviews and comparison shop.

CHAPTER 3
Ingredients Make the Maker

One of the critical components of your soap is the actual ingredients you select and use in your recipes. When we discuss ingredients this includes: lye, oils, butter, scents, additives and colorants. Each one will make an impact on the outcome of the final batch and each one can make or break an entire recipe.

As handcrafted soap making gains in popularity more exotic ingredients are introduced on the market. This is where you will need to exercise a little discernment or you run the risk of stockpiling 20 different molds, 50 different oils and 100 different fragrances in your soap room. Many of these ingredients will either expire before they can be used or fail to live up to the hype. Not every oil is created equal and this is also true for suppliers.

Remember what you put into the soap pot literally comes out in the wash, if you skimp on quality ingredients it will show in your final bars. Listed below are the basic staple ingredients every soap maker should have in their soap room.

- ☐ Sodium Hydroxide
- ☐ 1-2 Gallons of Distilled Water
- ☐ Olive Oil
- ☐ Castor Oil
- ☐ Coconut Oil
- ☐ Shea Butter
- ☐ Cocoa Butter

- ☐ Palm Oil

*Optional Ingredients
- ☐ Soap Colorant
- ☐ Essential oils or Fragrance oils of your choice

There is no magic bullet for finding the perfect color or scent. Soap making is scientific and there is always a bit of chemistry at work. Color and scent is where much of your trial and error will come into play.

Whenever you are trying a new ingredient, start small. Many suppliers offer discount based on the quantity of what is ordered. What good is it to save money if you hate the ingredient?

It's perfectly fine to buy base ingredients like lye and base oils in bulk but you must remember that EVERYTHING has a shelf life and an expiration date. It's not saving if you end up wasting the ingredients. A general rule of thumb is if you can't use it within 3 months…don't buy it.

When I first started making soap, I would stockpile ingredients because I knew "at some point" I would use it. I just wanted to have it on hand "just in case". Needless to say, my some point never came to fruition and I had to toss the expired ingredients. If you want to start wasting money, start stockpiling ingredients and watch those expiration dates creep up ever so quickly. If you don't have an immediate need, don't buy it.

You can find a list of reputable Soap Suppliers at: **https://livesoapschool.com/recommendedsuppliers**

CHAPTER 4
Lye aka Sodium Hydroxide

If I had a dollar for each time someone asked "Can soap be made without lye?", I would easily be a millionaire. There's not a live stream or local soap making class I have completed where this question doesn't invariably appear. Luckily I've been streaming for a while and many of my regular viewers are able to answer the question before I even see it. If you are reading this book you may not have seen a live stream so I'll explain further.

Sodium Hydroxide is used to make hard bar soap. Potassium Hydroxide is used to make liquid soap. Both Sodium Hydroxide and Potassium Hydroxide are commonly referred to as lye. Lye is required to create the chemical reaction known as Saponification. If you don't use lye, you don't get soap. Have you ever tried to mix oil and water? It just doesn't work. The only exceptions to the rule are premade melt and pour glycerin soap where the manufacturer has already completed the saponification process with the lye for you.

Soap is made by combining oils and fats with a lye solution. This forces the chemical reaction known as Saponification. As long as the recipe is formulated appropriately, there will be no lye in the final batch of soap.

<u>The trick is for you to exercise proper safety precautions when using Sodium Hydroxide. All the Time!</u>

Respect the Lye and You Have Nothing to Fear

Lye is a caustic and corrosive substance in its raw state. You must be careful and protected when working with it. As long as you follow basic soap safety measures, you will be fine working with Lye.

What does it mean to be safe with lye?
Always wear gloves and goggles when working with lye and soap batter.
- ☐ Gloves protect your hands in the event of splashes
- ☐ Safety Goggles protect your eyes

If you get lye or raw soap batter on your skin, DO NOT PANIC. Rinse the area with cold water. It can be extremely dangerous if you splash lye in your eye as it can lead to blindness. I'm not saying this to scare you I'm saying this because it's true and so that you will ALWAYS wear goggles. You should also consider wearing long sleeve shirts, pants and closed toe shoes as protection for your skin.

The next time someone asks you can soap be made without lye, you can confidently respond NO. The question that usually follows is will there be lye in the soap once it's ready? Once again you can confidently answer no…as long as you used proper recipe measurements and followed the soap making procedure. There will be no lye in the final batch of soap.

You can watch a step by step soap safety demo at: https://livesoapschool.com/ingredients-to-success-resources/

CHAPTER 5
Scenting Your Soap

Essential oils and Fragrance oils are used to add scent to your soap. Some people even comment on the aroma therapy properties of bathing with scented soap. This is another part of the chemistry and artistry of making your own soap.

The scientific aspects consist of:

- How scent interacts with the other ingredients in your recipe
- How scents may impact the batch of soap
- How the scent may change over time

The artistic components include: your selection of scent and how it engages the senses.

Essential Oils

According to Wikipedia, "An essential oil is a concentrated hydrophobic liquid containing volatile aroma compounds from plants. Essential oils are also known as the oil of the plant from which they were extracted, such as oil of clove. An oil is "essential" in the sense that it contains the "essence of" the plant's fragrance."

Since these oils come from the plant, they are considered natural in your recipes. There is no chemical alteration that occurs aside from the distillation process used to extract the oil.

Some of the most common essential oils used in soap include: lavender, tea tree, rosemary, eucalyptus, cedarwood, patchouli, sage, peppermint, basil and frankincense.

This is just a starter list. Be sure to check the indications for each essential oil and consider mixing your own creative blends based on your own taste.

Fragrance Oils

According to Wikipedia, "Fragrance oil(s) are also known as aroma oils, aromatic oils, and flavor oils, they are blended synthetic aroma compounds or natural essential oils that are diluted with a carrier like propylene glycol, vegetable oil, or mineral oil".

This means fragrance oils are chemically altered or diluted. So unlike essential oils these are no longer considered natural. Many people choose to use fragrance oils in their soap because they are less expensive or to get a scent that is not economically available in an essential oil.

Scent Usage Rates in Soap

There is no hard and fast rule on the amount of essential oils and fragrance oils that you can incorporate in your soap recipe. The manufacturers of the oil will also include usage guidelines on the packaging or on their websites.

In cold process soap, the scent is added at trace, just prior to pouring the batter into the mold. This means that your fragrance or essential oil will come into contact with your lye solution. We generally need more scent in cold process soap to account for this interaction with lye.

The general rule of thumb is to start with .5 to 1 ounce of scent per pound of oil used in your recipe. If you were using 2 pounds of oil in your recipe you would use up to 2 ounces of fragrance or essential oil to scent your soap. You can always adjust up or down depending on your preference. Just be aware that the scent may fade, morph your colors or change over time as chemistry is still at work.

Two Considerations When Working with Scents

Flash Point

Each fragrance oil and essential oil has a flash point. This is the temperature where the scent will evaporate because it is too high. Since you are working at very high temperatures you be sure to check the flash point of your selected fragrance or essential oil.

When you are ready to add the scent to your soap mixture, check the temperature to make sure your beautiful smell doesn't disappear because of the flash point.

Discoloration
Discoloration occurs when fragrance oils or essential oils have vanilla in the ingredients. Vanilla is naturally brown and therefore it will change the color of your soap to a darker shade.

When you are creating an intricate design with several bright colors the worst thing that can happen is it suddenly changes to dark brown. You will sadly watch your hard work disappear. To prevent this from happening you can use a vanilla stabilizer or avoid fragrance oils with vanilla in them all together. Also testing a fragrance in a small batch is a good way to determine how it will react with color.

Selecting Scents for Your Soap
This is yet another million dollar question…Which scent should I use? Unfortunately and fortunately, there is no one right answer. There are thousands of scents available on the market. This is another place where trial and error becomes your friend.

As you are starting out, buy small sample sizes of the fragrances from reputable suppliers. Make sure the scents are bath and body safe or soap specific fragrance oils. Test them in your recipes and get feedback from friends and family.

You should always try to test new ingredients, including fragrances and essential oils in small batches. Once you have a basic recipe that you love with minimal ingredients, use this as your standard test recipe as well. By having a standard test recipe you will know how it reacts normally. If any abnormalities occur, it will be evident and you will know what caused the changes.

This is a practice I often skip and inevitably end up paying for it later. I once tried to do a six color soap with a brand new fragrance oil. This fragrance was DEVINE to all the senses; I was beyond excited to get it in a batch of soap. The moment I added it to my mixture, it immediately turned into a thick and useless mess.

Did I mention I was making 10 pounds of soap? That's a lot of oil and a lot of money wasted. Had I just tested in a small batch, I would have known it wasn't a good fit. Use my experience as a constant reminder to always test new scents in small batches before committing to larger batches.

CHAPTER 6
Additives

Additives are any ingredients included in your soap recipe that are above and beyond the oils and butters in the base recipe. Additives can offer beneficial properties to the bar, texture or color. There is no one size fits all recommendation for additives and like everything else in soap making trial and error is going to offer you the best results.

To select your additives, begin by identifying the quality you are looking for and then match the additive that will impart that particular quality. Additives can be used to exfoliate, provide additional emollients, create a texture or even impart color in your soap recipes. Increasingly consumers are becoming more aware of ingredients and additives help your product standout for their natural abilities.

You will be surprised to discover that many of the items in your pantry can also be used as additives in your handmade soap recipes.

I'll offer one piece of advice here, not all additives are created equal. Be sure to do your research and remember that there is a chemical reaction occurring in the pot. With that being said not EVERYTHING is suitable for adding into your recipes.

Always test in small batches before committing your precious oils and butters in large batches. Additives are generally added at 1 teaspoon to 1 tablespoon per pound of oil. If you were making 2 pounds of soap you would use up to 2 tablespoons of your chosen additive. As you gain more experience you can adjust this up or down to suit your preferences.

Botanicals

Flower Petals, lavender buds, tea leaves and herbs all fall under the category of botanicals. While they are beautiful and can add a ton of character to your soap, they often turn to a dark black or brown color when coming in contact with your soap batter. To avoid this color change consider adding botanicals as decoration on the top of your soap.

Crushed or Ground Oats

Crushed and Ground Oats are the most common ingredients used to add exfoliation properties to soap because of their texture. You can use oats in their original state to add some dimension to the top of your soap or ground them into a fine powder that can be incorporated into the soap batter.

Poppy Seeds

Poppy seeds are another additive you can include in a batch of cold process soap. They provide some artistic character in the form of speckled dots as well as exfoliation power. If you add them to the top of soap, be sure to lightly push the seeds into the batter to avoid them falling off.

Honey & Sugar

Honey is a natural humectant which draws moisture to the skin. Both honey and sugar help to increase the lather of your soap however it also increases the temperature of the mixture. This increase in temperature can cause your soap to crack right down the middle. When incorporating honey in your recipe you want to work at low temperatures and consider placing your soap mold in the refrigerator for a few hours.

Milk

Milk adds moisture and gentle exfoliation to soap due to the fats, minerals and vitamins the milk contains. Two of the most popular milks used in soap making are goat and coconut milk. I've even heard of camel milk soap although I have never actually tried this in a batch of soap. Milk is typically added as the liquid portion of the lye solution and it's frozen, to prevent burning the milk causing a brown color. This is a pretty advanced method but I want you to be aware of this as an additive.

Activated Charcoal

One of the most popular and trendy additives on the market today is Activated Charcoal and for good reason. Due to the oxidation process the surface of the charcoal is able to trap toxins making it ideal for skincare. Activated Charcoal also creates a very rich dark grey to black color in soap. To incorporate in your soap, use 1 tablespoon of charcoal per pound of oil and add at trace. You can also mix your charcoal with a light oil to make it disperse easily.

CHAPTER 7
Recipes Create Balance

In order to progress as a soap maker and move beyond recipes found online, you must understand the properties of fatty acids found in oils and butters. Consider the spices in your kitchen cabinet; each one imparts a different flavor in your food. This is the same concept for soap making. Each oil is made up of different fatty acids which gives your final batch of soap a distinct "flavor".

Learn the qualities of each of the 8 fatty acids and the common oils where they can be found. Refer to the table below.

Fatty Acid	*Qualities in Soap*	*Common Oils*
Lauric Acid	Cleansing Hard bar Fluffy lather	Coconut, Babassu, Palm Kernel
Linoleic Acid	Conditioning to skin Creates a silky feel	Sesame, Hemp, Safflower
Linolenic Acid	Conditioning to the skin	Canola, Rice Bran, Sunflower
Myristic Acid	Hard Bar Cleansing Fluffy lather	Coconut, Babassu
Oleic Acid	Conditioning to skin Slippery feel Low lather	Olive, Sunflower, Canola
Palmitic Acid	Hardness Cleansing Steady & Creamy	Palm, Cocoa Butter

Fatty Acid	Qualities in Soap	Common Oils
	lather	
Ricinoleic Acid	Soft bar Conditioning to skin Moisturizing to skin Fluffy stable lather	Castor Oil
Stearic Acid	Hard bar Longevity of bar Steady lather	Soybean Oil, Mango Butter, Shea Butter

3 Steps to Get Started Creating Your Own Recipes

1. **Determine which oils contain the qualities you desire and their usage rates**

    Let's say that you are creating a moisturizing bar. You would look for two or three fatty acids that offer moisturizing qualities to your batch of soap. Then you identify oils that are high in those particular fatty acids.

2. **Understand that there is a trade off and you should aim for balance in your recipes**

    You will need to do a little juggling with your recipes and be willing to trade off for more of one over the other. The key is to try and achieve balance.

    Let's say that you really love olive oil because it is high in moisturizing qualities, there is nothing to prevent you from making a 100% olive oil soap (this is called castile soap).

The problem is it will have a very long curing period also; you give up luscious lather as olive oil fatty acid profile doesn't offer this quality. Instead you could look for complimentary oil like coconut oil to boost the lather and hardness of the bar.

3. Use a Soap Calculator

You provide percentages of the oils and butters you want to use and the soap calculator will provide exact measurements for each ingredient. Soap calculators do the math for you! They also can give you a pretty good idea of how your soap will perform, before making it. This is one critical step to ensure that you have the correct amount of lye and don't waste any ingredients. One very popular lye calculator can be found at **http://www.soapcalc.net**.

You can search online for step by step soap calculator tutorials and in-depth tutorials. Each one is a little different but they all complete the calculations for you. Part II of this book has several recipes to help you get started, even these you should run through a soap calculator to get in the habit of checking all recipes.

CHAPTER 8
Color Creates Character

When people pick up a bar of soap, there are several characteristics that make it unique. One such characteristic that truly catches the eye is the choice of color. Color helps to bring out the essence of the bar while also conveying its own style and the individuality of the soap maker. Many people will coordinate the colors with the scent of the soap to create an entire experience for the senses.

There is a wealth of options when it comes to coloring your soap and generally you will use micas or pigments. Some people even use natural colorants but that is outside the scope of this book, and there is currently some debate on whether or not they can be used legally. Take note that when you use mica colorant or pigments your soap is no longer considered 100% natural as these are considered synthetic ingredients.

Mica
This definition comes from one of my favorite suppliers for soap colorants Rustic Escentuals.

> "Mica pigments are the name of a group of natural occurring minerals which can range from being completely matte to sparkling or opalescent. Mica pigments are a purified and crushed mica mineral."

I prefer mica colorants for most of my soap projects as they create bright vivid colors. Mica colors can be mixed with oil, glycerin or water to help disperse it in your soap batter.

The usage rate for mica is generally 1 teaspoon of mica color per pound of oil. So if you have 4 pounds of oil in your recipe, you would use 4 teaspoons of mica colorant.

Pigments

Pigments typically come in powdered form. Soap pigments are approved for cosmetics and are purified and refined so they are safe to use on the skin. Oxides should be added with water to prevent a speckling appearance in your soap. Each manufacturer will provide guidelines for the usage amount of water to use with their particular oxide.

Starting Lineup of Colors

Micas and pigments can get very expensive. If you have to start with just a few, pick the primary colors

- Red
- Yellow
- Blue
- Titanium Dioxide for white

These colors can be used to make secondary colors. Also pick up some body safe glitter, as this can be used to decorate your soap as well.

How to add color to your soap

1. Measure teaspoons of color based on weight of oils and place colorant in a plastic container.

2. Add 3 times the teaspoons in water, light oil or glycerin to the container holding the colorant.
3. Mix well.
4. Once your soap mixture reaches a light trace add the color and mix well until it is completely incorporated in the soap batter.

A Note About Titanium Dioxide

Titanium Dioxide is used to color handcrafted soap white. It can potentially speed up the soaping process. Be sure that you allow yourself time to pour in the mold before it gets too thick.

The Color Wheel is your Friend

It can be very tempting to add every color to your batch of soap, if you do this you may be very disappointed to find that you end up with a brown murky mess. Utilize the color wheel to determine complimentary colors that will create designs that last beyond the soap pour.

NEVER USE FOOD COLORING IN YOUR SOAP!

This is not approved for bath and body products.

CHAPTER 9
Terms & Acronyms You Should Know

As you continue your research, interact with other soap makers and suppliers these terms are bound to come. I don't expect you to memorize these terms and acronyms but it is important for you to have a basic understanding of what each term means. These are just the tip of the iceberg as the soaping industry is constantly evolving.

Saponification
This is the scientific term for soap making. It is the chemical reaction that occurs when combining a base (fatty acid) with an alkali (sodium hydroxide) to produce a salt (soap) and a free alcohol (glycerin). If anyone ever asks you can say, it is the chemical reaction that requires sodium hydroxide to convert the oils into soap.

Lye
Another term for sodium hydroxide and potassium hydroxide, this is the alkali used to make soap. All soap making requires the use of lye.

SAP value
The number of milligrams of lye required to saponify 1 gram of fat. In other words this is how much lye is needed to convert 1 gram of particular oil into a salt. Every oil and butter has a unique SAP value.

Curing
The period of time after soap is unmolded to allow excess water to evaporate from the bar. Generally the cure time for cold process soap is 3 – 6 weeks.

Lye Heavy
Soap contains more lye than the fatty acids in the recipe and this excess lye remains in the final bar. This is unusable soap and must either be rebatched or tossed as it is not safe to use on the skin.

Water Discount
Reducing the amount of water required in the recipe. This is generally done to shorten the cure time for cold process soap or to account for additives that include water.

Super Fat / Lye Discount
When soap makers add extra oil to the recipe than what the lye will convert. This allows the extra fat to remain in the final bar as they are unsaponified. Super fatting is typically done to add additional moisture or cleansing to a bar while giving the soap maker wiggle room. The terms Lye Discount and Super Fat are often used interchangeably.

Trace
The point in soap making when mixture reaches a particular thickness or consistency is considered trace. There are several stages your soap will go through when mixing. First a light emulsification when oils and lye have just combined. Then it will move to light trace and finally a pudding consistency. Soap is poured in mold once it reaches trace.

Geling
When the soap mixture heats up and it looks translucent, this generally happens shortly after pouring into the mold or while sitting overnight.

CHAPTER 10
Time, Temperature and Trace

Three critical factors play important roles in your soap making process these are: time, temperature and trace. I often refer to these as the "Triple T" in cold process soap. Similar to cooking the time and temperature have a direct relationship with how smoothly your process will flow as well as the final outcome of your batch of soap. In my first book, *The New Soap Makers Cookbook – Ingredients for Success,* I briefly touched on the recipe of patience and this is where you will need it.

Time & Temperature
You must allow your ingredients time to cool. When you first create your lye solution it can go as high as 200 degrees Fahrenheit. If you try to make cold process soap with a lye solution this high, be prepared to run into trouble.

If you choose to melt your ingredients you must do so slowly, as this will ensure that the qualities of the oil don't burn off. Allow yourself plenty of time for all of your ingredients including the lye solution and melted oils to get to an appropriate temperature before commencing the soap making process.

Some soap makers will make soap when their ingredients are at 140 degrees Fahrenheit. This is considered high temperature soaping. Others will make soap when their ingredients are at room temperature (less than 80 degrees Fahrenheit). My preferred method is room temperature.

I have found that this gives me the most amount of time to work with my ingredients and I experience less cracking down the center of my soap AND I get less soda ash on the tops of my bars.

I would recommend that you give it a try at 4 different temperatures: room temperature, 100 degrees, 120 degrees and even 140 degrees if you are brave. I recommend you do this as experience is always the best teacher. You can take note of how your soap reacts and determine for yourself what your own preference is. Cold Process soap making depends on temperature and constant contact, what temperature is up to you as the maker.

Cold process soap also requires time to cure. This is the period after unmolding where you allow the excess water to evaporate out of the cut bars. If you attempt to short change this process your bars will not last as long and if you are selling your soap, your customers will notice.

Trace
I'm not really sure where the term trace was coined but trace was one of the trickiest things for me to understand when I first started making soap. Did my soap actually reach it? Was it ready to be poured? Could I mix a little more? Most descriptions of trace are when you lift your stick blender out of the mixture you are able to see a light trail remain on top of the batter. This is considered the point in soap making when mixture has completely mixed and is ready to be poured.

Trace is important because it indicates that your oils and lye have fully combined in the pot and have a better chance of not separating in the mold. However trace can be a delicate situation if you are attempting intricate designs or working with tricky scents or additivies. Depending on the design you are attempting you may need a very thin trace or even a very thick trace to achieve distinct layers.

Similar to the temperature it's best to try mixing to various levels of trace to see what works best for you and your recipes. As long as your oils and lye solution are completely mixed, you will end up with soap. The designs you are able to achieve will be dependent on the level of trace you allow your soap mixture to reach before pouring into the mold.

CHAPTER 11
Preparing to Make Soap

There is one critical piece we must cover before we move on to the steps to actually make soap and that is your preparation. Preparation can make or break your experience in so many ways. The more prepared you are the easier it will be to deal with unexpected surprises or how smoothly your process will flow.

Time is not on your side once you get started, by being prepared you can maximize the time you do have focusing on your soap making and not looking for supplies, ingredients, additives, molds or your fingers. Ok not your fingers but hopefully you get my point.

This is the routine I use each time I start a new soaping project. Consider adapting for your own soaping adventures.

- ☐ **Lay out all of your supplies and ingredients**
  By having everything within arms reach in your workspace you will not have to stop midway through the process to locate anything. This includes your recipe, scales, mixing bowls, spatulas, soap mold, all ingredients including additives, colorants and scents. Consider creating a checklist of basic supplies and refer to this each time you begin a new project.

- **Suit up for Soap Safety**
  You will be working with sodium hydroxide which is highly corrosive in its original state. Your oils, butters and soap batter will be very hot. If this splashes on you it can be a very serious burn or worse. To protect yourself and your eyes, commit to always wearing gloves and goggles each time you make soap.

- **Measure Ingredients Before Starting The Stick Blender**
  All oils, butter, lye and water should be weighed by weight and not volume. This means you must use your scale to weigh each ingredient. This ensures you are getting an accurate calculation for the saponification process. Be sure to measure everything before you start mixing as you may not have time to stop and measure once you get started. This is especially true for your scents and colors.

CHAPTER 12
The Steps To Make Soap

The steps to make cold process soap are pretty straight forward. These are the steps I follow when making cold process soap. Remember it is very important to keep safety in mind. Make sure you are wearing goggles and gloves to prevent burns in the event of splashing or spills. Also do not use any aluminum or cast iron for your soap making as it will not end well. Make sure you have all of your necessary supplies before beginning the process. With your recipe in hand follow the steps below.

1. Put on your gloves and goggles before getting started.

2. Weigh Sodium Hydroxide in a cup on your scale.

3. Weigh Distilled Water in a plastic pitcher on your scale.

4. Slowly pour the Sodium hydroxide into the pitcher of water **(Do not pour water into sodium hydroxide)**

5. Stir the sodium hydroxide and distilled water until the solution becomes clear, set aside to cool. (Do not stand right over the pitcher as it will release fumes that can be irritating if inhaled)

    pour slowly & stir slowly

6. Measure your oils and butters in a large mixing bowl or stainless steel pot.

Always water first; Lye second
① set up water 32
② set up Lye last

7. Melt your butters over a low flame on the stove or in the microwave in 45 second intervals to avoid overheating.

8. Check the temperature of lye solution and oils. Once they reach less than 100 degrees Fahrenheit you can move on.

9. Slowly pour the lye solution into the melted oils and give it a quick stir with your spatula.

10. Continue to mix the combined solution with your stick blender until it reaches a light pudding like consistency (this is trace).

11. If you are adding color to your soap, separate your batter into individual bowls and add your premixed color. Use a spatula to fully incorporate the color with the batter. If needed, use your stick blender to ensure the color is fully mixed in.

12. If you are adding scent to your soap, pour the essential oil or fragrance oil into the batter and use your spatula to mix well.

13. Pour the soap mixture into your mold and give it a light tap on the table or on the floor to prevent air bubbles. You can also use a small mallet to tap the sides of the mold as this will help to pop any air bubbles that formed when pouring your soap batter.

14. Spray the top of the soap with 91% rubbing alcohol to prevent soda ash (a white powdery looking substance that is harmless but impacts the appearance of soap.)

15. Cover the soap mixture with saran wrap or plastic wrap.

16. Insulate with a blanket or towel and allow the soap to sit for 24 hours.

17. Unmold your soap, and cut into the desired bars.

18. Allow your soap to cure for 4 to 7 weeks to allow any excess moisture to evaporate and ensure you have a firm mild bar of soap.

19. Test the pH level of your soap to ensure that it does not contain any excess lye.

20. Weigh the same bar of soap each week. Each week you will notice that it loses weight. Once it stops losing weight, your soap has fully cured.

21. Enjoy the fruits of your labor with a warm bath or a nice shower using your handmade soap.

CHAPTER 13
Get Yourself a Soap Notebook

You have just made ten batches of soap and four of them are amazing. Your co-worker loves the one that smells like cranberries. Your family can't get enough of the one that looks like a lemon cake. That swirl is INCREDIBLE, but how did you make it? Can you recreate it? Which one did you add that extra ingredient, what scent is in there, what temperature did you soap at? Which recipe was it?

I am sharing this lesson from personal experience. I had a total of 25 recipes and none were quite the same. My Lemon Meringue Pie was an instant hit with everyone who tried it. One problem, I didn't know which of my recipes created it. I had two choices: recreate each one or bite the bullet and create a new recipe. I went with option two and I'm still not 100% positive that the results are the same.

I said all of this to say, it's very important to create a soap notebook and keep good notes on each recipe you make. It is very important for any experimental process to be able to retrace your steps if you ever hope to recreate it. Or, at the very least, to backtrack enough to know what went wrong and what could have caused it. This becomes more in the realm of possibility with an accurate soap notebook. Now you can see the level of importance that the detailed notation of each recipe could have on unlocking your signature style, techniques and recipes.

The more detailed your notes, the easier it will be to repeat or tweak as necessary.

CHAPTER 14
Troubleshooting Problems

I just took my soap out of the mold but the top has this thin white film. What is it?

What you may be noticing is soda ash. This appears as a thin layer of white dust on the top of your bars. The good news is it's harmless and purely aesthetic. The bad news is if you worked really hard on fancy swirls and designs it can get lost under the ash. To prevent soda ash from forming, after pouring your soap into the mold liberally spray 91% rubbing alcohol on the top and cover with plastic wrap.

Soda Ash is caused by the lye interacting with the air. By spraying with alcohol and covering with plastic wrap you are limiting the exposure to air. If you still get some soda ash on the top of your bars and want to remove it, simply apply some steam and wipe it with a towel. Or leave it be and allow the true handcrafted nature of your soap to shine through.

My soap is really sticky and it is sticking to the side of my mold. Is there any way to harden it up?

> You should check your recipe to ensure that it is balanced and doesn't contain too many soft oils. You can try adding Sodium lactate to your recipe as this helps with hardening soap and with releasing from the mold.

I found a recipe that I like but it calls for palm oil can I just substitute palm kernel flakes?

Palm kernel flakes and palm oil have very different chemical make ups and therefore have different SAP values. Remember the SAP value is the amount of lye needed to convert the oil. If you simply substitute the oil without reformulating the recipe, you will run into problems and potentially end up with lye heavy soap. This can easily be avoided.

This goes for all oils and all recipes you find online and in books. Always run a recipe through a soap calculator to confirm the proper measurements for your ingredients. Then and only then can you be certain that why you put in the soap pot will be saponified properly.

My soap has a long crack down the middle, what causes this?

>Your soap got too hot in the mold while it sat overnight. If you added sugar or honey to your batch, consider placing in the fridge for a few hours as these ingredients typically heat up a batch. Also consider soaping at lower temperatures. This is purely aesthetic and you can attempt to fix it by simply pressing the soap together.

As I was mixing my soap it got very thick and it started to look grainy.

>The chemicals in your fragrance oil may cause your soap batter to start getting thick very quickly. This is called acceleration. Your soap batter may get rock solid immediately, also known as soap on a stick or seizing. Your batter may even look like it has rice throughout the mixture referred to as ricing.
>
>For this reason I always recommend testing any and all new fragrance oils in small batches of soap.

Part II
Cold Process Soap Recipes

What would a cookbook be without recipes? In the next section I list some of my favorite recipes that you can try at home. These recipes are meant to introduce you to the simplicity of soap making while not overwhelming you with expensive or unnecessary ingredients. The primary purpose of these recipes is to give you a starting point with ingredients you should be able to find easily.

The recipes are presented in two formats: percentages and 2 pound batches. I provide the recipes in this manner in case you want to scale up or down, you would simply use the percentages for each ingredient in an online soap calculator instead of the exact measurements. If you want to just get started with small two pound batches I have done the calculations for you and provided the exact weight for each ingredient.

For each recipe, follow the steps outlined in the Steps to Make Cold Process Soap chapter.

CHAPTER 15
Basic Soapers Recipe 3 for 3

This is a basic starter recipe that will give you a nice hard bar of soap that lathers beautifully. Many soap makers will begin with this recipe if they want to use minimal ingredients with a quality bar of soap to show for it. I also like this recipe as a base testing recipe when testing new fragrances and colors.

RECIPE:

This recipe will yield 2 pounds of soap:

- ☐ Sodium Hydroxide – 86 grams
- ☐ Distilled Water – 224 grams
- ☐ Olive Oil – 200 grams
- ☐ Coconut Oil – 195 grams
- ☐ Palm Oil – 195 grams

If you would like to use a lye calculator to adjust the size of the recipe the percentages are listed below.

- ☐ Coconut Oil -33%
- ☐ Palm Oil – 33%
- ☐ Olive Oil – 34%

CHAPTER 16 Simple Soap

A gentle bastille soap is great for sensitive skin and babies. It only uses three ingredients and is known to be very mild. Due to the high percentage of olive oil in this recipe it may take a while to come to trace just remain patient and continue to stir until you get to the pudding like consistency.

RECIPE

This recipe will yield 2 pounds of soap.

- ☐ Sodium Hydroxide – 82 grams
- ☐ Distilled Water – 224 grams
- ☐ Olive Oil – 413 grams
- ☐ Coconut Oil – 147 grams
- ☐ Castor Oil – 29 grams

If you would like to use a lye calculator to adjust the size of the recipe the percentages are listed below.

- ☐ Olive Oil – 70%
- ☐ Coconut Oil – 25%
- ☐ Castor Oil – 5%

CHAPTER 17
Lots O' Lather

Sometimes you just want to see a ton of suds when you lather your soap. This is a great cleansing bar due to the high content of lather producing oils.

RECIPE
This recipe will yield 2 pounds of soap:

- ☐ Sodium Hydroxide – 85 grams
- ☐ Distilled Water – 224 grams
- ☐ Coconut Oil – 177 grams
- ☐ Palm Oil – 165 grams
- ☐ Olive Oil – 147 grams
- ☐ Cocoa Butter – 71 grams
- ☐ Castor Oil – 29 grams

If you would like to use a lye calculator to adjust the size of the recipe the percentages are listed below.

- ☐ Coconut Oil -30%
- ☐ Palm Oil – 28%
- ☐ Olive Oil – 25%
- ☐ Cocoa Butter – 12%
- ☐ Castor Oil – 5%

CHAPTER 18
Essential Bar

One of the most popular and easily recognizable scents in handmade soap is Lavender. This recipe incorporates lavender essential oil, mica colorant and lavender buds to create a truly luxurious bar of soap that's alluring on all of the senses. You can substitute your favorite essential oil blend for the lavender if you choose.

RECIPE

This recipe will yield 2 pounds of soap:

- ☐ Sodium Hydroxide – 85 grams
- ☐ Distilled Water – 224 grams
- ☐ Coconut Oil – 177 grams
- ☐ Palm Oil – 165 grams
- ☐ Rice Bran Oil – 147 grams
- ☐ Mango Butter – 71 grams
- ☐ Castor Oil – 29 grams
- ☐ Lavender Essential Oil - 1 ounce
- ☐ 2 teaspoons of purple mica
- ☐ 2 teaspoons of lavender buds

If you would like to use a lye calculator to adjust the size of the recipe the percentages are listed below.

- ☐ Coconut Oil -30%
- ☐ Palm Oil – 28%
- ☐ Rice Bran Oil – 25%
- ☐ Mango Butter – 12%
- ☐ Castor Oil – 5%

After sprinkling your lavender buds on top of the batter, be sure to use a skewer or chopstick to lightly push your lavender buds into the soap to prevent them from falling off.

CHAPTER 19
White Soap

This recipe produces a white bar of soap because there is no olive oil in it. This bar is also very cleansing and conditioning. This is great to use when you are attempting to achieve vibrant colors as you are starting with a white base. Don't worry it may look yellow as you are mixing, once it cures it will be white unless you add color.

RECIPE

This recipe will yield 2 pounds of soap:

- ☐ Sodium Hydroxide – 83 grams
- ☐ Distilled Water – 224 grams
- ☐ Coconut Oil – 177 grams
- ☐ Castor Oil – 41 grams
- ☐ Sunflower Oil – 88 grams
- ☐ Rice Bran Oil – 283 grams
- ☐ Optional – 1 ounce Essential oil or Fragrance oil

If you would like to use a lye calculator to adjust the size of the recipe the percentages are listed below.

- ☐ Coconut Oil -30%
- ☐ Castor Oil – 7%
- ☐ Sunflower Oil – 15%
- ☐ Rice Bran Oil – 48%
- ☐ Essential oil or fragrance oil of your choice – 1 ounce per pound of oil

CHAPTER 20
Charcoal Soap

Activated charcoal is extremely cleansing. It's a natural ingredient that is becoming widely known for its ability to draw toxins to the surface of the skin.

RECIPE

This recipe will yield 2 pounds of soap:

- ☐ Sodium Hydroxide – 81 grams
- ☐ Distilled Water – 224 grams
- ☐ Coconut Oil – 117 grams
- ☐ Palm Oil – 11 grams
- ☐ Rice Bran Oil – 236 grams
- ☐ Sweet Almond Oil – 88 grams
- ☐ Castor Oil – 29 grams
- ☐ 2 Tablespoons of Activated Charcoal Powder
- ☐ 1 Ounce of Peppermint Essential Oil

If you would like to use a lye calculator to adjust the size of the recipe the percentages are listed below.

- ☐ Coconut Oil -20%
- ☐ Palm Oil – 20%
- ☐ Rice Bran Oil – 40%
- ☐ Sweet Almond Oil – 15%
- ☐ Castor Oil – 5%
- ☐ 1 Tablespoon of Activated Charcoal Powder per pound of oil in your recipe
- ☐ 1 Ounce of Essential oil per pound of oil

Once your soap reaches a thin trace and you have added your essential oil, separate batter into two separate containers. Add the activated charcoal to one of the containers and mix well. Pour one layer of the soap into the mold and alternate back and forth to create layers. Allow to sit in mold overnight, cut and cure following the steps to make soap.

CHAPTER 21
Poppy Exfoliation

Poppy Seeds offer a speckling exfoliating character in your soap. This recipe combines this with the wonderful fragrance of Grapefruit essential oil. You can substitute the fragrance oil with your favorite scent.

RECIPE

This recipe will yield 2 pounds of soap:
- ☐ Sodium Hydroxide – 81 grams
- ☐ Distilled Water – 224 grams
- ☐ Coconut Oil – 117 grams
- ☐ Beef Tallow – 11 grams
- ☐ Rice Bran Oil – 236 grams
- ☐ Shea Butter – 88 grams
- ☐ Castor Oil – 29 grams
- ☐ 2 Tablespoons of Poppy Seeds
- ☐ 1 Ounce of Grapefruit Essential Oil

If you would like to use a lye calculator to adjust the size of the recipe the percentages are listed below.
- ☐ Coconut Oil -25%
- ☐ Beef Tallow – 30%
- ☐ Rice Bran Oil – 25%
- ☐ Shea Butter – 15%
- ☐ Castor Oil – 5%
- ☐ 1 Tablespoons of Poppy Seed per pound of oil in your recipe
- ☐ 1 Ounce of Essential oil per pound of oil

Once your soap reaches a thin trace, and you have added your scent pour your premeasured poppy seeds into the batter. Mix well to incorporate thoroughly. Pour your soap batter into the mold allow to sit for 24 hours before cutting and curing.

CHAPTER 22
Clay Soap

Clay can be incorporated in soap recipes to impart detoxifying qualities and extra absorbency for impurities. What makes them so unique is that they can also add a silky feel to your bars. Depending on the color of the clay, your soap will naturally inherit beautiful shades of color from the clay. You can use bentonite clay, kaolin clay, or rose clay for this recipe.

RECIPE

This recipe will yield 2 pounds of soap:

- ☐ Sodium Hydroxide – 85 grams
- ☐ Distilled Water – 224 grams
- ☐ Babassu Oil – 177 grams
- ☐ Sweet Almond Oil – 165 grams
- ☐ Rice Bran Oil – 147 grams
- ☐ Cocoa Butter – 71 grams
- ☐ Castor Oil – 29 grams
- ☐ 3 Tablespoons of Rose Clay
- ☐ 1 Ounce of Lemongrass Essential Oil

If you would like to use a lye calculator to adjust the size of the recipe the percentages are listed below.

- ☐ Babassu Oil -30%
- ☐ Sweet Almond Oil – 23%
- ☐ Rice Bran Oil – 30%
- ☐ Cocoa Butter – 10%
- ☐ Castor Oil – 9%

☐ 1.5 tablespoons of clay per pound of oil in your recipe & 1 ounce of scent per pound of oil

CHAPTER 23
Cup O' Joe

Coffee is great at absorbing odor and it has a very distinct smell. If you have a coffee drinker in your life, Cup O' Joe soap will be perfect for them. For this recipe you will need extra strength fresh brewed coffee and coffee grounds. You will substitute brewed coffee for the distilled water portion of the lye solution

RECIPE
This recipe will yield 2 pounds of soap

- ☐ Sodium Hydroxide – 82 grams
- ☐ Brewed Coffee – 224 grams
- ☐ Olive Oil – 413 grams
- ☐ Coconut Oil – 147 grams
- ☐ Castor Oil – 29 grams
- ☐ 1 ounce of Eucalyptus essential oil or 1 ounce of vanilla fragrance oil (note that vanilla fragrance oil will color soap brown this may be a good or bad thing depending on your design)

If you would like to use a lye calculator to adjust the size of the recipe the percentages are listed below.

- ☐ Olive Oil – 70%
- ☐ Coconut Oil – 25%
- ☐ Castor Oil – 5%
- ☐ Use Brewed Coffee in place of the water
- ☐ 1 ounce of essential oil per pound of oil in your recipe

CHAPTER 24
Sea Salt Spa Escape

The Sea Salt Spa Escape recipe will give you a spa like bar that is hard and exfoliating due to the salt content. The only salt you cannot use in your soap recipe is Dead Sea salt as this salt is known to make your soap cry... Not necessarily tears but it will look like it's weeping. Salt is known to be a lather killer so we combat that by increasing our coconut oil and super fatting at 20% to prevent a drying effect caused by too much coconut oil.

RECIPE
This recipe will yield 2 pounds of soap:
- ☐ Sodium Hydroxide – 81 grams
- ☐ Distilled Water – 243 grams
- ☐ Coconut Oil – 472 grams
- ☐ Shea Butter – 29 grams
- ☐ Castor Oil – 88 grams
- ☐ 14 ounces of Himalayan Sea Salt
- ☐ ½ Ounce of Rosemary Essential oil
- ☐ ½ Ounce of Lemon Essential oil

If you would like to use a lye calculator to adjust the size of the recipe the percentages are listed below.
- ☐ Coconut Oil -80%
- ☐ Shea Butter – 5%
- ☐ Castor Oil – 15%
- ☐ 70% of your oil weight for Himalayan Sea Salt

Once your soap reaches a light trace, add the Himalayan Sea Salt to the batter and pour into the mold. It should harden within 4 or 6 HOURS so be ready to take it out quickly. Consider using individual cavity molds to help release the soap quicker. Allow to cure normally.

CHAPTER 25
Final Thoughts for New Soap Makers

Well you've made it to the last chapter and I want to share a few final thoughts with you. These thoughts come from countless conversations with new soap makers as well as my own experiences as a handcrafted soap artisan.

Learn to trust your instinct

Your experience will be your best teacher. While many soap makers can share their lessons learned and experiences, you won't truly understand until you experience it for yourself in the soap pot or in the mold. Allow that same curiosity that got you started with the craft to be your fuel when the soap doesn't turn out exactly as expected. There is always a lesson in the mess. Look for it!

No two soap makers are the same

Be kind to yourself as you are getting started and try not to get in the habit of comparing yourself to others. Beauty is in the eye of the beholder and that's not just a saying. It's 100% accurate. No two soap makers are alike and that is the beauty of it all. You get to create something with your own two hands, and use it on a daily basis. How many things in your home have you made, that you get to use every day?

Safety is NOT optional
There are basic and serious safety guidelines for working with lye, essential oils and soap batter. If you commit to adhering to the soap safety guidelines *every time* the soap world becomes your oyster. If you choose not to adhere, well it will become your soap disaster.

Perfection is an illusion and Curiosity Fuels Creativity
There is never one perfect way of doing something and the only way to truly experience the craft is to learn the basics and commit to pushing the limits of your own creativity. When you find yourself saying *"what if I tried…"* or *"what if I added…"* Do a little research and go for it. These simple questions will lead you to your unique style and some incredible creations. Know that you will make mistakes, we all do. Use each mistake to hone your craft and explore further.

Patience is a virtue
Patience is going to be your most tested virtue and here is why.
- You should test in small batches before committing to larger batches…this requires patience
- You must wait for the appropriate temperatures before you can begin…this requires patience
- You must wait 24 to 48 hours before you can cut your soap…you guessed it, patience
- You have to wait four to eight weeks before you can actually use the soap (no cheating)…yep more patience
- You will wait patiently and not so patiently for supplies to arrive if you order online

You should eliminate can't from your vocabulary and commit to trying it. You may surprise yourself and find that it's actually possible. Don't be surprised if everything you see on a daily basis becomes your next inspiration for soap. I wish you much success in your new soaping adventure.

-SoapLadyZ

Stay Connected

Stay up to date on the blog at LiveSoapSchool.com

Zakia blogs regularly with lessons learned, how-to's and live streams at livesoapschool.com. Subscribe today and stay up to date on the latest episoaps.

Let's Get Social

 Join us at **facebook.com/livesoapschool** to catch our next live stream and ask questions live.

 Join Zakia live for daily live vlogs on twitter at **twitter.com/zakiaringgold**

 Follow Live Soap School on Instagram for DIY tips, soap inspiration and behind the scenes tutorials at **instagram.com/livesoapschool**

About the Author

Zakia Ringgold is the Owner of Natural Soap By Zakia and Creator of Live Soap School where she teaches people around the world the art and science of soap making. She truly enjoys motivating and inspiring others to unlock their creativity through the craft of making soap.

What seemed as art therapy for Zakia was the beginning of her Handmade Soap Business. To Zakia, soap making is a form of alchemy – transforming the oils into something of value while instilling a sense of confidence in the creator. Soap making is about awareness, empowerment and creativity. To her, it is so much more than soap. As such a portion of each bar sold is reinvested in after-school programs teaching kids in the community to make their own bath products.

Zakia lives and streams in Philadelphia, PA with her two daughters: Nyla and Paige. Nyla practices her singing and dancing while Paige makes her own version of soap pies right alongside mom while broadcasting Live.

Additional Reading

Need even more inspiration? Zakia is the author of another cookbook which lays the foundation for successful soap making. In *"The New Soap Makers Cookbook: Ingredients for Success"* you will discover key recipes that most soap makers stumble over when getting started and when attempting to grow their craft. You can find this book on **Amazon** and on the website at **LiveSoapSchool.com**.

Made in the USA
Monee, IL
17 May 2021